Overcoming Ahithophel Syndrome

A Guide to Forgiveness

Diana Spencer

DAYELight
PUBLISHERS

ISBN: 978-1-949343-86-1 (paperback)

Acknowledgement

The unmerited love of God that He continues to bestow each day is all I need to survive the storms in this life. I thank God for His unwavering love and patience with me over the years. I thank Him for the Holy Spirit who speaks to me and gives inspiration daily.

I want to thank my husband and soul mate, Andrew, for his invaluable support in everything pertaining to me. Your motivation and encouragement have driven the process of completing this book.

Thanks to my children, Rebekah and Josiah, who inspire me to be my best self for them to emulate.

Thanks to my dad and mom, Clinton Williams and Dorrett Lawrence Williams, who have been my cheerleaders since birth; love always.

Thanks to all my siblings and other family members. Life is greater and more colourful with you being a part of it.

Thanks to all my friends who have been there over the years and who have helped me through difficult moments in my life. Your words of encouragement and prayers have kept me.

Thanks to my "Andrews" family; our bond of over twenty-four years is a testament of true friendship.

Thanks to my church family for helping me to grow spiritually and for all the love and support.

Thanks to the team at DayeLight Publishers, in particular, Crystal, for her professionalism and competence in bringing my book to life.

Table of Contents

Introduction

Every good gift and every perfect gift is from above, and cometh down from the Father of lights, with whom is no variableness, neither shadow of turning. (James 1:17).

God has given us many gifts to enhance our lives and one such gift is forgiveness. He knows the unsurpassed pleasure that comes from showing compassion. The inspiration to birth this book, "Overcoming Ahithophel Syndrome: A Guide to Forgiveness" was placed on my heart by God. Several years ago, while living in the Bahamas, I spent a lot of time in devotion to God. While going through the Scriptures, I met Ahithophel who could be described as a minor character with a major message. He stood out in my mind and for several weeks I was not able to shake the thought of the events of his life. Little did I know that after several years the Lord would have used Ahithophel through this medium to bring glory to His name and to lead His people on the path of forgiveness.

This book gives a sneak peek on a bit of my life growing up and how that has shaped my personality and walk with God. It provides an overview of the life of King David and how he has dealt with seeking God for forgiveness for the wrongs that he had done and also for God's support in getting him through problematic seasons in his life, while exercising forgiveness towards those who have done him wrong.

David and Ahithophel chose different ways to deal with their anxiety, hurt and frustration and the results were strongly evident. This book also explores the importance of love and how it transcends any conflict that we may face. Love coupled with the Word of God is a great tool needed to help us to live rewarding lives. You may be having problems with your neighbour, a friend that you hold dear, your children, spouse, a family member, a colleague at school or work, church brethren or a stranger. They may have done things that seem unforgivable, unexpected or inexcusable. It might be a case where you have ignored your feelings of resentment and while you try to get along with the individual, your heart is full of disdain. Maybe you have not spoken to your offender for years but every time you remember the incident you become uneasy and angered. Is it a case where you ignore the phone calls of the wrongdoer as you tell yourself "once bitten, twice shy?" Maybe you have never met the person, but you wish that karma would do its job. This, I describe, as "Ahithophel Syndrome" or one who suffers from "Ahithophelia."

Forgiveness is God's ointment that He has given to alleviate our vicious emotions and set us free. This book is geared towards encouraging us to turn to God and intentionally

8

seek Him to learn the art of forgiveness, and then relax in the beauty of the fullness of life through the grace of God. At the end of this book, you should be encouraged to take the necessary steps to forgiving someone who has offended you.

Foreword

*A*hithophel *Syndrome* captures the heart and soul of the author on matters that we all confront daily. As far as hearts and souls go, there is no cleaner heart or purer soul that would be more qualified to guide us along a path of self-improvement and forgiveness. Diana's honest and sincere insights take us to a place that we never knew existed, in much the same way that most readers were unaware of such a Bible character. The author beautifully weaves a web that enables us to be transported from a place of longing and non-acceptance to a destination of forgiveness and amazing growth.

We are skillfully awakened to the consciousness that no relationship, career, financial status or popularity can create the ultimate "safe haven" for us. Wherever we find happiness, it is always interrupted by a failure in people or systems. No position or possession in this world will ever truly allow us to feel the joy and peace that Christ has to offer. We can be happy for a while but there is always a feeling that something is missing. For many persons, that feeling of emptiness cannot be satisfied with all they acquire, hence some people turn to drugs and illicit lifestyles that mask the symptoms but never truly heal them.

This exploration reveals the essence of much of our existence and Diana Spencer delves beneath multiple layers to unearth a reality that only in Jesus can this complete healing be found. She, however, does not do this in the usual traditional way that Christian inspirational books normally do, but rather bases the entire thesis on the unique experience of a relative unknown in the Scriptures. Though of unknown measure, he was connected professionally and personally to one of our favourite Bible characters, "the man after God's own heart," David. This is compelling for several reasons. On the one hand, his station might have offered opportunities for what many of us today would consider fulfilling. On the other hand, it makes the reader ask the question, "How could I not have known him?" Both observations are also emblematic of our own unconsciousness of our weaknesses and shortcomings.

What the author accomplishes in this book is expertly making the reader come to a point of recognition through the lens of her own life and development; a talent that only a few authors have mastered with such seamlessness. She shares the story of her struggles, which take on a different complexity at varied stages in her growth. She also shares her triumphs over these obstacles in a very passionate, rational, and Biblical exposition, which allows the reader to extract tools for their own victories. Most notably, Diana tackles the complex matter of forgiveness, not from the

12

usual point of condescension and austerity, but with a candid look at the challenges inherent to forgiveness. She then untangles the yarn of how to navigate those complexities.

All in all, I am happy to have read the text because, most importantly, it has made me a better person. My joy, however, is further multiplied to know I have such brilliance so close to me.

My dearest wife, Diana, has put into writing the encapsulation and embodiment of the fighter and ultimate winner that she has become. Most profoundly she convinced me through the reading that I can do it too. No doubt, you will be as convinced as I am. This MUST READ, is transformative from start to finish and has the power to empower not just Christians, but people from all walks and from many nations.

Dr. Andrew Spencer

" GOD DOES NOT GUARANTEE US A LIFE FROM TROUBLE, BUT HE DOES PROMISE TO BE OUR REFUGE IN THE MIDST OF THE STORM.

~ EXCERPT FROM GOD IS MY REFUGE

chapter 1

Safe Haven

We often find our emotions changing, depending on the situations, circumstances, stages, and moods that we experience. We question our abilities, or lack thereof, our existence, purpose, and means to achieve what we want. This is how we live and thrive daily. For many people, stability is something they only dream about as life is filled with its challenges that require solutions, unfortunately, out of reach.

I was a happy child growing up. I was in a stable enough home, with both parents around, along with siblings who were colourful and unique in their own way. Giggles came so naturally to me; after all, I was the baby of the family and was certainly protected. Life indeed was a "safe haven."

By age eleven, my perspective on life had turned in another direction. I had to live without some of my siblings, who had migrated or moved out to live on their own. At that point it was my fifth year of living in a multi-family housing arrangement, also known as a "tenement yard." Life was about to throw its many darts at me, that in some cases were just too hard to dodge.

That chapter in my life lasted for fifteen years and, at the end of it, I learned some life lessons that shaped who I am as an adult. I learnt how real the teachings of the Bible are when it speaks about jealousy, maliciousness, anger, idolatry, hatred, and group rivalry (See Galatians 5:20) and how important it is to honour your parents (See Exodus 20:12). You see, I have been in situations where my family was attacked numerous times by people who were simply jealous and hateful. We were labelled as workers of witchcraft because we were thriving in school; the neighbour called her dog by the first name of my dearest family member; my brother was spat at in the face; urine was thrown at my feet; my sister was gossiped on, lied on and hated by those around. Life had become too burdensome and overbearing that my giggles literally disappeared as misery took a toll on my spirit and existence.

I became more reserved and was often extremely quiet at school, not being able to relate to my friends who were always trying to support my unpleasant moods. They knew they had done nothing wrong, so after some time they would ignore my sad disposition as I tagged along with them throughout the day. One friend sat with me in silence and was never bothered too much that I was not in the

17

mood to share what I was going through at home. My friends became my "safe haven."

I thank God today that He is an awesome God who has always been watching over this little sparrow, long before she even met Him or understood the importance of serving Him. I thank God He provided a "safe haven," which taught me Biblical principles before I even knew they existed. He taught me that:

> *"An angry man stirreth up strife, and a furious man aboundeth in transgression."* (Proverbs 29:22).

> *"Let all bitterness, and wrath, and anger, and clamour, and evil speaking, be put away from you, with all malice."* (Ephesians 4:31).

> *"Make no friendship with an angry man; and with a furious man thou shalt not go: Lest thou learn his ways, and get a snare to thy soul."* (Proverbs 22:24-25)

> *"Deceit is in the heart of them that imagine evil: but to the counsellors of peace is joy."* (Proverbs 12:20).

Since high school, I have had several experiences and met countless individuals. However, my friends remained in my life even when we were thousands of miles apart. Having friendships extending beyond twenty-one years is a huge blessing and should be treasured.

18

In every situation, though, even the best friendships that we have are often tested by life's woes. We reflect at times and wonder how our relationships became sources of terror in our lives based on simple disagreements or differences in our ideologies. We try our best to hold on to the past; reminiscing on how healthy our friendships were and wish we were able to mend them with ease. We invest a lot of time and energy in other people's lives because we love and care about them too deeply to see them hurt. Unfortunately, people hurt us in different ways when we leave ourselves vulnerable to them. Sometimes we find ourselves in terrifying circumstances that are no fault of our own and we wonder, "How did my life end up this way?" The truth is, once we exist, we will have problems that we may not be able to fix.

Even after I met Christ and started to walk with Him, I did not understand how to give Him my burdens. I recited and believed that I was: *"casting all my cares upon Him"* (See 1 Peter 5:7). However, several years after professing my faith, I realized that I was far from giving Him my worries and fears. I often tried to fix my problems in ways I thought were best. Even at times when I prayed, I brought my strategies to God requesting of Him to work through my plans to fix the situations. Frustration set in when, after many attempts, the situation kept escalating, spiralling out of my control.

It is interesting how we can live for Christ but not grasp the principles that He has provided for us to live a fulfilling life.

One day, while praying, I found myself asking God to take over and bring me through my problems. I was sincere in my request and I felt a peace that calmed my spirit and allowed joy to set in, even when the problems still existed. God is truly a burden-bearer, the only One who can refresh us and make us peaceful when our world is chaotic.

As a parent, the responsibilities become greater each day as we fight against what our children are exposed to at an early age. My husband and I became strategic with teaching our seven-year-old daughter the principles that would make her a vessel for Christ. This was not always easy, neither could we achieve this on our own, so we consistently prayed and laid our daughter at the mercy seat of Jesus. As parents, we should not feel the need to do it alone or pretend as if we know all the answers. Our source of strength and reliability is Christ Jesus. We also believe that if we train our daughter well, she will be an example for her younger brother to follow.

Experiences over the years have taught me that no relationship, career, financial status or popularity can create the ultimate "safe haven" for us. Wherever we find happiness, it is always interrupted by a failure in people or systems. No position or possession in this world will ever truly allow us to feel the joy and peace that Christ has to offer. We can be happy for a while but there is always a feeling that something is missing. For many people, that feeling of emptiness cannot be satisfied with all they acquire, hence, people turn to drugs and illicit lifestyles that mask the symptoms but never truly heal them.

Jesus wants us to recognize that He is our "safe haven." Matthew 11:28 testifies to this as Jesus offers us a place of rest: *"Come unto me, all ye that labour and are heavy laden and I will give you rest."* When I was seeking after Christ, this verse gave me strength and conviction. The world had thrown its weight on me in many forms and I was carrying it around daily, sometimes feeling sorry for myself and wondering if my future will ever get any better. But I finally answered the call of Jesus, as He had been knocking on my heart's door for some time. It was the best decision I ever made in my life. There is simply no greater satisfaction than accepting Jesus as your greatest love. He simply makes all the other loves in your life worthwhile. He will teach you to love beyond your spouse, children, relatives and friends. You will learn how to truly love openly as Jesus did, sacrificing and never expecting any favour in return. He will make you have compassion for strangers who you have never met. Your heart will enlarge with a love that is boundless.

You may say only Jesus can love that well or we were not made with such capacity. This is not true, for Jesus admonishes us to: *"Love each other as I have loved you."* *(John 15:12).* Some people who profess Christianity make it hard for non-believers to accept Christ because they do not apply the principles given. We find that many Christians are hateful, lacking purity of heart and are not mindful of others' feelings. It becomes hard for those looking for a change in their lives to turn to Jesus because they believe that no real change can happen since poor behaviours in Christians are becoming the norm.

I had some harsh experiences being a part of the body of Christ. People carry around troubling issues that can affect your spirituality without any fault on your part. Our minds are constantly bombarded with issues from all aspects of life and we tend to forget who is our "burden bearer." This is how we unconsciously invite the devil into our thoughts to ultimately dictate our actions. There were occasions when I questioned my role and existence in the body of Christ. I remember sharing with some friends that the interaction at church was not quite pleasant, but I loved the worship.

I soon realized that worship was enough to keep my mind in perfect peace. If you can find the true reason why you decided to walk with Christ, He can deliver you from any uncomfortable situation and is able to guard your heart. He says: *"Thou wilt keep him in perfect peace, whose mind is stayed on thee: because he trusteth in thee."* (Isaiah 26:3). Over time my passion grew from worship sessions to learning and understanding the Word of God. Bible Study became a great need for me as the Word began to be inscribed on my heart. My appetite for understanding the teachings of Jesus grew stronger daily. There was no other way to fulfil this need but by prioritizing time for Christ.

We must be mindful not to be trapped in the notion of believing that attending church is enough for us to live for Christ. He wants us to seek after Him daily (See 1 Chronicles 16:11). God intended to meet with man in the Garden of Eden daily (See Genesis 3:8). We can create our own garden for God to meet us in. The day I decided to spend at least one hour each day in devotion with God was one of the best decisions I ever made since my walk with Christ. I spoke to God and told Him my desires to seek after Him. I wanted to learn more about His ways, His love, His mercy, the things that displease Him and those that make Him happy. I wanted to understand the heart of God.

My first challenge was to read the entire Bible within a year. At the beginning it felt as if I was only reading stories but after a while the Bible started talking to me. I then recognized that God was using His Word to change my life. It became less about knowing the characters and more about the lessons to be learnt, the call of God on my life and the different ways I can please Him. I started to develop a change in value. I started to decrease as God increased in my life. I understood that it was not about me, it was never about me. Yes, He wants His children to be happy and fulfilled but His glory in all our accomplishments must be honoured above all things.

Jesus gave us advice about the way to His Father's heart. He says: "...*I am the way, the truth, and the life: no man cometh unto the Father, but by me.*" (John 14:6). There are countless examples that Jesus left for us to follow. He loves

OVERCOMING AHITHOPHEL SYNDROME

us so much that He knocks at our heart's door. If we take some quiet time for Him, we will hear the knocking grow stronger. He understands all that we go through and our nature to sin but if we believe in Him, true repentance can take place. His journey on earth was never easy and He never proclaimed that if we live for Him, life would be easy. But He promised us that He will give us joy, even in our worst situations.

In Matthew 8, we are told about a disciple who requested some time to go and bury his father. Verse 22 says: *"But Jesus said unto him, Follow me; and let the dead bury their dead."* For some time, I tried to understand the meaning of this. What was Jesus saying here? Was He not in tune with the disciple's sorrow? It captured my attention and I thought about it for a long time. After months of reading and reasoning in my heart, the light bulb moment came. It was not about Jesus being indifferent to the situation, but rather He knew something that the disciple did not. Jesus knew that when we serve God, do His work and worship Him, He will give us joy. So, although the disciple was in the middle of grief and, no doubt, pain for his loss, God was saying to him, keep concentrating on Me, keep doing My work, keep worshipping Me, keep focusing on Me, and I will swap your sorrow for joy.

My point is, whatever you face in your life, however difficult and unforgiving it may seem, keep your focus on Jesus, "let the dead bury their dead" and walk in the newness of God's grace. Your soul will be lifted to higher levels in Christ. It simply means you have no vacation days when you live for God. It is not wise to be so overwhelmed with problems that you crawl under a sheet and stop worshipping God. Whatever your mission is, continue to do it, even when it hurts.

What is your "safe haven?" Is it your job, home, friends or family? Have you ever truly experienced joy without Christ? Jesus is our ultimate "safe haven" and without Him all other areas in our lives exist with varied moments of happiness that last only for a short time. God wants you to make Him your "safe haven" so you will experience joy that will sustain you, even when you are going through the worst trials in your life.

NOTES

_____

_____

_____

_____

_____

_____

_____

_____

_____

_____

_____

_____

_____

_____

_____

_____

_____

_____

"" STRENGTH AND COURAGE AREN'T ALWAYS MEASURED IN
MEDALS AND VICTORIES. THEY ARE MEASURED IN THE
STRUGGLES THEY OVERCOME. THE STRONGEST PEOPLE
AREN'T ALWAYS THE PEOPLE WHO WIN, BUT THE PEOPLE
WHO DON'T GIVE UP WHEN THEY LOSE.

~ ASHLEY HODGESON

chapter 2

Sin Devises
Strategies

n our efforts to remedy our problems, we naturally do what we think would make the situation disappear. Sometimes our intentions might be pure but, in some cases, mixed with anger and revenge. When revenge is in our hearts, we find ways to hurt others so we can feel satisfied that the individual pays for what we went through. Many may never admit to having such a view on life because it makes them look evil in the eyes of others and we care a lot about people's perception of us. The cunning and crafty plans that we devise in our minds eventually turn into actions as our hearts become less in tune with the other person's feelings or situation, while self-gratification becomes our priority. We elevate ourselves most in these situations, as we believe that justice should be served and no one else truly knows how we hurt deeply. We also have those individuals with very pure intentions to fix their own problems, which, however, becomes disastrous.

Proverbs 3:5-6 cautions us to: *"Trust in the Lord with all thine heart; and lean not unto thine own understanding. In all thy ways acknowledge him, and he shall direct thy paths."* God knew we would have problems that we are unable to fix on our own and He also knew we are naturally sinners so evil will prevail at times.

In the Bible, we meet David from he was a little boy protecting his sheep and, thereafter, defeating Goliath to bring victory to his people. We see God raise up David as a King and declare that he was *"a man after His own heart"* (See Act 13:22). David was devoted to God and spent a lot of time in reverence to Him. He was also repentant (See Psalm 25:11). It was evident that David and God had a beautiful relationship. David learnt that it was not a good thing to live in a sinful state but to acknowledge his sins and ask God for forgiveness. As Christians, at times we get distracted and are thrown off from fulfilling our purpose in God. David was also guilty of this.

In 2 Samuel 11, we were told that David was to go to war, but he stayed behind. While on his roof, he saw Bathsheba and he enquired about her. Although David heard that she was Uriah the Hittite's wife, he sent for her still. After having an adulterous tryst with Bathsheba, she became pregnant and sent this message to David. David immediately tried to devise a plan that would correct his sin. He sent for Uriah, who was at war. His intention was for Uriah to become intimate with Bathsheba so the baby could be passed off as his own. However, Uriah was a very

29

dedicated soldier and believed that it was dishonourable for him to have pleasure, while his comrades were risking their lives fighting. When David realized that Uriah would not copulate with his wife, he wrote a letter and gave Uriah to deliver to his captain. This letter held the instruction for Uriah to be placed at the front of the battle, while his fellow soldiers would retreat, leaving Uriah to die. David contrived this entire plan to cover his sins. However, his strategy was unsuccessful, as people in the palace knew all that was going on. There is always someone watching us, even when we are unaware. Later, the prophet Nathan visits David (2 Samuel 12:1-7) and tells him a story of a poor man who had an ewe lamb that he adored. Now a rich man had a visitor, so he took the man's one ewe lamb and prepared a meal, instead of choosing from the many lambs he had. When David heard this, he got so upset and said: *"the man that hath done this thing shall surely die" (Verse 5).* Nathan then reveals, *"Thou art the man" (Verse 7).* Sin is never satisfied. David had many wives, so he had no need to send for Bathsheba. In the end David repented and although God spared his life, He allowed the baby to die.

One could say that sin is very selfish and gives no thought to all who might be affected. When we become creative in strategizing to cover our wrongs, we affect many people, some of whom we may be unaware of. Have you ever noticed that people with no common interest or those who hate each other are able to become immediate friends, if they have a common enemy? I have seen this type of behaviour in people many times. Sometimes it is also difficult to detach emotionally from another person's hurt, especially when that person is close to you.

It was interesting to see a trusted adviser giving Absalom very bad advice that would hurt David. His loyalty for David had switched as he continued to work closely with Absalom. In this case he had his own agenda and sought to hurt David as much as Absalom did. He therefore gave Absalom ill advice, which pushed him to totally dishonour David, his father (See 2 Samuel 16:21). This otherwise noble man told Absalom to place a tent on top of the castle where he could share intimacy with all of David's concubines, thereby defaming the king (See 2 Samuel 16:22). It must be noted that this same man was David's adviser, an upright person, who had an impeccable reputation up to that point. In 2 Samuel 16:23, we were told that Ahithophel's counsel: *"was as if a man had enquired at the oracle of God."* This, in simple terms, means that when he gave advice in those days, it was spot on. When he had spoken to both David and Absalom, it was as if it came from the throne room of God.

This was a wicked act from someone David trusted. Ahithophel became an angry, unforgiving, and hurtful person. He was no longer David's counsellor. David, in 2 Samuel 15:31, was told that Ahithophel was among those who conspired against him. David then prayed to God to *"turn the counsel of Ahithophel into foolishness."* In 2 Samuel 17:1-3, Ahithophel told Absalom to give him twelve thousand men and he would kill David. Surprisingly, his counsel was questioned for the first time as Absalom sent for Hushai, who revealed that Ahithophel's counsel was "not good" (2 Samuel 17:5-7). Absalom listened to Hushai instead of Ahithophel; God had answered David's prayer. Ahithophel realized that it was all over for him as no one trusted him, so he went home and hanged himself (2 Samuel 17:23).

When I was first introduced to this character, I became increasingly curious as to why he would move from a state of being described as a spokesman for God (enquired at the oracle of God), one who is honoured and respected, to one who committed suicide. Ahithophel's journey did not make much sense to me until I delved deeper into the Scriptures and then realized that he was a man who was deeply wounded, angry and bitter.

What could have caused Ahithophel to become so bitter that he ended his life? When it became public knowledge that David had taken Bathsheba and had destroyed her family, it was thereafter that Ahithophel began to counsel Absalom. In 2 Samuel 11:3 and 23:34, it became clear that Bathsheba was the granddaughter of Ahithophel. He lost a wonderful grandson-in-law; he lost a great grandbaby and he had to witness the shame that Bathsheba went through.

I wondered how Ahithophel must have felt when his grandchild was defiled by David or when his noble grandson-in-law had been murdered innocently. He was so close to the king, yet the king betrayed him and destroyed

32

his family. Ahithophel was greatly affected by David's actions and he had some choices to make. He could either devise strategies to hurt David or allow God to work on his heart and help him to forgive David.

Suicide should never be an option for us, no matter what people have done to hurt us. Nothing is worth us losing our lives over. The bitterness that exists was formed because we were wounded over some things that were said or done to us. Sometimes we tell ourselves that we have forgiven, however, we avoid the individual at all costs: we don't take their phone calls, we don't want to hear their names and we continue to have bad thoughts about the individual as we repeat the situation in our minds. We hold on to things without seeing the need to let go and truly experience the power of forgiveness.

While hoarding ill feelings about others, we essentially poison our minds with toxins that are deadly for our health. We often hear that our state of mind can trigger various illnesses. Anger, maliciousness, having a sense of loss, annoyance, doubt, jealousy, guilt, depression and envy are just some of the negative emotions that can be devastating when they are left to become a part of our core (Hoffman, 2017).

These emotions force even the best of us to expedite tactics that are far removed from Christ. We easily blame people for some of the choices we make and how we react in various situations. We gain comfort by passing the blame, but we must always be accountable for our actions. Always know that you have a choice so there is no need to react impulsively to someone who has done you wrong. However, the right reactions are never easy for some of us to display, so we need the love and strength of God to restrain and direct us. We must fight against our natural state and reach out to God for an intervention. With Him out of the situation, we are bound to do the wrong things and lose out on the joy that is divine.

Maybe you had situations in your life where you were hurt. Perhaps it was your child, parent, spouse or a friend who was hurt. You are probably having sleepless nights, thinking about the situation and becoming bitter towards the individual at fault. Remember, once we start nurturing bitterness, we have already sinned and sin devises strategies to committing even more sins. So, while you believe you are hurting someone else, what you are essentially doing is hurting yourself and the people you love most.

NOTES

ADVERSITY IS THE DIAMOND DUST HEAVEN POLISHES ITS JEWELS WITH.

~ CORRIE TEN BOOM

chapter 3

Ignoring Survival Instincts

I recently attended a high school graduation, where Dr. Spencer taught the graduates that they must develop a strong core to survive. He emphasized that "your stomach must be strong to make it in this tough world." He went on to explain that it is important to have that core because life will throw many obstacles in our way and if we cannot find our centre, we will be lost. These few words stayed with me long after that function as I reflected on the many times I had to fight to make it through challenging days and seasons in my life. He also spoke about using our minds to control our willpower, as it all begins with our thoughts. I am sure that many can identify with this as the Bible rightly encourages us to: *"be ye transformed by the renewing of your mind."* (See Romans 12:2).

God understands that our strengths reside in our mind. If we have faith and think positively, we are already winners.

38

When we depend on God, He will give us the ability to formulate survival tactics. We can develop survival instincts by using our minds to develop our core. I believe we were all born with instincts that help us as babes to find our mother's chest at feeding time or to cry as soon as we are left alone in a room. We want to be held and comforted as if our inner being somehow knows that it is important to feel protected.

As we grow older, we learn many survival skills based on our socialization. Some may have been in situations where they had to make escapes to keep their lives, while others were mostly sheltered. Whatever the circumstances we all had, it is an innate impulse to put up a fight when we feel threatened.

There are those, at some point, who have decided that life is too unbearable and, therefore, choose to die. This desire becomes domineering the more they ignore their survival instincts. Ahithophel had opportunities where he could seek God and find that peace within to help him get over his dark emotions. Instead, his mind was engrossed in finding ways to pacify himself by hurting David. The more he planned against David, the more a piece of him was eaten away and destruction became his friend.

He first started to die spiritually as his moral compound and love for God became as vapour and vanished. Darkness and devastation crowded his mind, drowning his thoughts and erasing all the will he had to live. I am sure we all had moments where we were so upset that all we fixated on was finding our own solutions and forgetting, in those moments, to seek God for guidance. Luckily, the Holy Spirit speaks to our consciences and moves us to cry out to God.

When we have no desire to pray and dwell in the presence of God, that is a good sign that we are ignoring our spiritual instincts to survive. If we are not careful, we will soon indulge in activities that are far from Christ, thus commit spiritual suicide. This is where the devil wants us to be so he can destroy us. Building our resistance against these desires is what we must train our minds to achieve. 1 Peter 5:8–10 tells us to: *"Be sober, be vigilant; because your adversary the devil, as a roaring lion, walketh about, seeking whom he may devour: Whom resist steadfast in the faith, knowing that the same afflictions are accomplished in your brethren that are in the world. But the God of all grace, who hath called us unto his eternal glory by Christ Jesus, after that ye have suffered a while, make you perfect, stablish, strengthen, settle you."*

It is never easy to build resistance, especially when it is natural to do wrong. In order to survive, our endurance in Christ must be strong and deeply anchored. Do not be confused and believe we can achieve this on our own because it can only be done with the help of the Holy Spirit. You will survive, if you recognize how easy it is for you to lose your way in serving God. Once we are conscious of this possibility, then we can identify the little things that are placed in our lives by the devil to derail us. This type of attitude and awareness will help us to never ignore our survival instincts.

Personally, I have learned to build resistance by exercising my spirituality. I acknowledge that my life belongs to Christ and it is a commitment that I have made for the rest of my life. Thoughtfully, I have moved from creating a fad about serving God, to developing patience in living for Jesus. In my early Christian years, my enthusiasm for Christ was short-lived with periods of sad and doubtful moments, which robbed my chance of experiencing the fullness of His joy.

Over the years my spirit longed for completeness in Christ. While praying and sharing this desire, I conceded that I had to build some muscles:

ఞ **Faith Muscles:** Developing faith is a very arduous task, as it takes fortitude through the Word of God. One must acknowledge the power of the written Word of God and believe in Him simply because He says so. It is reminding yourself of the many times God has not left you alone and the many times He took you out of harm's way. We will know that our faith muscles are in-tact when we remain firm in Christ and are able to worship through our difficult times. When we learn from our tough experiences and trust God to take us through it and not out of it, then we know that we are exercising our faith.

∽ **Prayer Muscles:** This muscle formation takes patience and a realization of the importance of communication with God. Firstly, one must never perceive that you must kneel by your bedside or enter into a spiritual realm to pray. If you accept that prayer requires simplicity and genuineness, then it will not be deemed as a task. Wherever you are, there is full access to Christ and, therefore, it is very easy to talk to God. Speak to Him from your heart as you would when expressing yourself to the closest among you. Although He knows what bothers you, even more than yourself, still tell Him and ask for peace and clarity of the mind. When you feel guilty about being too busy to talk to God or when you reach a place where no matter what is happening around, you have an earnest desire to talk to God, then you know that your prayer muscles are maturing.

∽ **Charity Muscles:** *"Charity suffereth long, and is kind; charity envieth not; charity vaunteth not itself, is not puffed up. Doth not behave itself unseemly, seeketh not her own, is not easily provoked, thinketh no evil; Rejoiceth not in iniquity, but rejoiceth in the truth; Beareth all things, believeth all things, hopeth all things, endureth all things."* (1 Corinthians 13:4–7). This Scriptural passage demonstrates that love is full of action and character. An individual is only able to love through expressions and deeds. Once we have love, it cannot be kept to ourselves or be silent; it must be encouraged to speak. Its voice should reach beyond our families and friends and should touch people who we have not met or those who are our enemies. Love simply cannot ignore the needs of others around us. Instead, it finds ways to assist. Therefore, if you find yourself seeking God on others' behalf and thinking of creative ways to assist others, leaving behind revengeful thoughts, then our charity muscles are progressing.

Developing all confidence in God and learning to relax in His favour is another survival strategy that we can develop, knowing that He is deliberate and will always do things to demonstrate His glory. Putting aside our own desires and acknowledging that it is God's purpose that will prevail, then His sovereignty will lead our existence daily.

As we make a choice to not only exist but to live spiritually, we must ensure that His presence resides with us. Hence, we must endeavour to worship Him continuously, which helps to clear your mind of evil thoughts and fill it with hope; the means to survive.

NOTES

" ESSENTIAL TO RECEIVING DIVINE FORGIVENESS ARE
PERSONAL, INDIVIDUAL RECOGNITION AND ACCEPTANCE
OF OUR FATHER'S MERCY, MADE AVAILABLE TO US BY
THE ATONING SACRIFICE OF JESUS CHRIST AND A
RENEWED COVENANT TO OBEY THE PRINCIPLES OF THE
GOSPEL.

~ RONALD E. POELMAN

chapter 4

Accepting Christ's Forgiveness

ow remarkable and refreshing it is to know that we serve a living God who is too holy to dwell in our darkness, yet magnificent in His power and willingness to forgive us of all our sins. People shy away from serving God because they believe their sins are too big for God to grant them a reprieve. Isaiah 1:18 reminds us that God is ready to forgive us this very second. He says, *"Come now, and let us reason together, saith the Lord: though your sins be as scarlet, they shall be as white as snow; though they be red like crimson, they shall be as wool."* All one needs is a penitent heart for God to shower us with His compassion. But although God is ready to forgive us, He also requires us to become better stewards for Him.

Although we know that God does not expect us to become sinless, we should not use this as an excuse to say, "God understands." Notwithstanding, it is important to lose the fallacy that you have too many sins for God to forgive. Proverbs 24:16 states, *"For a just man falleth seven times, and riseth up again: but the wicked shall fall into mischief."* David was the epitome of a righteous man and received forgiveness countless times from God. What was interesting in the story of David is the fact that he was always remorseful and was able to acknowledge his sins and ask God for pardon.

The popular Psalm 51 demonstrates David's penitence as he made this prayer after his sins were revealed to him by Nathan the prophet, according to the will of God. David knew the severity of the situation and submitted to God's will as his child died. David wrote this heartfelt passage, pleading to God for mercy and forgiveness as he earnestly laments over his sins: *"Have mercy upon me, O God, according to thy lovingkindness: according unto the multitude of thy tender mercies blot out my transgressions. Wash me throughly from mine iniquity, and cleanse me from my sin. **For I acknowledge my transgressions: and my sin is ever before me.** Against thee, thee only, have I sinned, and done this evil in thy sight: that thou mightest be justified when thou speakest, and be clear when thou judgest. Behold, I was shapen in iniquity; and in sin did my mother conceive me. Behold, thou desirest truth in the inward parts: and in the hidden part thou shalt make me to know wisdom. Purge me with hyssop, and I shall be clean: wash me, and I shall be whiter than snow. Make me to hear joy and gladness; that the bones which thou hast broken may rejoice. Hide thy face from my sins, and blot out all mine iniquities. **Create in me*** *a clean heart, O God; and renew a right spirit within me. Cast me not away from thy presence; and take not thy holy spirit from me.* Restore unto me the joy of thy salvation; and uphold me with thy free spirit. Then will I teach transgressors thy ways; and sinners shall be converted unto thee. Deliver me from bloodguiltiness, O God, thou God of my salvation: and my tongue shall sing aloud of thy righteousness. O Lord, open thou my lips; and my mouth shall shew forth thy praise. For thou desirest not sacrifice; else would I give it: thou delightest not in burnt offering. **The sacrifices of God are a broken spirit: a broken and a contrite heart, O God, thou wilt not despise.** Do good in thy good pleasure unto Zion: build thou the walls of Jerusalem. Then shalt thou be pleased with the sacrifices of righteousness, with burnt offering and whole burnt offering: then shall they offer bullocks upon thine altar." (Psalm 51:1-19 – emphasis mine).*

As we continue to examine the conversation that Nathan had with David, it is observed that although God had forgiven David, He made him suffer the consequences of his actions. Not only did He take the child away from them but He also revealed that: *"......the sword shall never depart from thine house; because thou hast despised me, and hast taken the wife of Uriah the Hittite to be thy wife."* (2 Samuel 12:10). David was very humble in his reaction to Nathan and immediately confessed: *"I have sinned against the Lord"* (2 Samuel 12:13).

It is important to differentiate between forgiveness and punishment, for they are not the same. Forgiveness deals directly with the nature of the relationship between God and individuals and God demonstrated this by reinstating the relationship between Him and David. Nevertheless, the punishment follows as an indicator that all actions have consequences. David suffered tremendously for his mistake as the "sword" continued to work in his house. As we read in 2 Samuel, David's beautiful daughter called Tamar was raped by her brother Amnon, one of David's sons (See 2 Samuel 13). Absalom was deeply hurt by the occurrence, so he killed his brother Amnon. Thereafter, Absalom devised many strategies to overthrow David, his father, and take his kingdom. Many battles were lost, and David kept away as he hid from Absalom to preserve his life. Throughout all that he faced, David learnt much about accepting God's forgiveness and he taught us that we should:

- ᴥ Humble ourselves before God in everything and God will continue to be faithful. David exhibited this very well (See Psalm 51:17).

- ᴥ Accept the Lord's punishment without complaints. David never fostered anger against God. Instead, he prayed and kept a contrite spirit.

- ᴥ Continue to worship God. Remember, we do not take vacations from living for God. David continued worshipping God throughout his ordeal.

49

- ↣ Love the commandments of God and meditate on Him daily. David explicitly voiced this in Psalms 119:47-48: *"And I will delight myself in thy commandments, which I have loved. My hands also will I lift up unto thy commandments, which I have loved; and I will meditate in thy statutes."* It is evident that David, through continuous meditation, grew stronger in God and made the commandments his foundation.

- ↣ Praise God with thanksgiving. David admonishes us to: *"Enter into his gates with thanksgiving, and into his courts with praise: be thankful unto him, and bless his name."* (Psalms 100:4).

- ↣ Be confident that God loves you. David knew that God loved him, even when he sinned and walked contrary to His Word. David penned this thought well in Psalm 136:26: *"O give thanks unto the God of heaven: for his mercy endureth for ever."*

While David was busy repenting and learning to accept God's forgiveness, Ahithophel was drifting further away from the presence of God. As his distracted mind focused on hurting David, he lost his identity in God. Ahithophel did not have a desire to dwell in the presence of God and to be reassured that God is able to take control of any situation and that it is necessary to accept God's forgiveness for all the anger he festered in reaction to David's selfish actions.

To accept God's forgiveness, one must become apologetic about their thoughts, words and deeds. It is an entire reconstruction of our attitudes and values. Once we continue to work on applying justice in our own way, we become less interested to accept pardon from God. Receiving His forgiveness means letting go of the situation completely, giving it over to God and depending on His strength to support us. It also means forgiving yourself.

Even when God assures some of us that we have been forgiven, we find it difficult to forgive ourselves. We hold on to the guilt of our past downfalls and wallow in self-pity. To truly appreciate God's forgiveness, we must forgive ourselves. I know it is challenging at times, but it requires patience, empathy and love. Talking to God about your doubt, guilt and fears will help you to release it over time. Making a conscious effort to break away from self-pity and build self-worth can very much help in this regard.

Sometimes when we look back on our past, we become ashamed and settle into a state of humiliation, not allowing ourselves to learn from our mistakes and to find the will to keep close to God. Some may have the idea that God will never forgive them because of how "big" their sins are. You might be saying: "I have committed a sin that God won't forgive me for" or "Satan has kept me away from God for so long, it's just too late" or "I am not worthy of God's forgiveness."

In 1 Timothy 1 the Apostle Paul was a murderer who made it his duty to bring God's people to Jerusalem to be stoned to death. He labelled himself as the chief of sinners, but God saved him, and he accepted His forgiveness. Verse 16 says: *"Howbeit for this cause I obtained mercy, that in me first Jesus Christ might shew forth all longsuffering, for a pattern to them which should hereafter believe on him to life everlasting."* Paul is saying he is a perfect example of one who accepted God's forgiveness and became a powerhouse for Christ.

While Ahithophel remained infuriated with David, God already forgave David and was dealing with the situation as He saw fit. This is a constant reminder to us that we need to allow God to take care of our problems, as the offenders might unknowingly accept Christ's forgiveness, while we drown in an ache for revenge and obsession over gaining justice for what was done to us.

Are you willing to accept God's forgiveness today or will you stay bitter, while everyone is moving forward in God's glory? Right now, where you are, breathe a word of prayer and ask God to help you to release all the anger and hurt bottled up inside. Tell Him you are willing to give up on fighting this very moment and you are asking for forgiveness for even the malicious thoughts in your mind of which you are unaware. As you say this prayer, be willing to accept the Lord's forgiveness. He wants us to embrace His mercies. Remember, God works on a repentant heart, so be determined in your pursuit to embrace God's forgiveness and to be an example of how transformation is possible by the grace of our Father.

NOTES

_____

_____

_____

_____

_____

_____

_____

_____

_____

_____

_____

_____

_____

_____

_____

_____

_____

_____

_____

" IT'S NOT ABOUT **HOW MUCH** YOU DO, BUT **HOW MUCH LOVE** YOU PUT INTO WHAT YOU DO THAT **COUNTS.**

~ MOTHER TERESA

chapter 5

Choose Love and
Hone it

My older sister shared a personal story with me about the many challenges she faced with a friend. She said: "In life, you have to choose to love and I chose to love my friend no matter what." While these lines lingered, every other word became muffled, and my mind would not allow me to move on. She was correct; love is a choice to make. We choose to love our families, friends, spouses, neighbours and strangers. Love is based on you and not on someone else.

If we, therefore, choose to love someone, we are then able to forgive them, though it might be difficult. Making that conscious decision to choose love will help us to go to the source of love in all situations. 1 John 4:7-8 says: *"Beloved, let us love one another: for love is of God; and every one that loveth is born of God, and knoweth God. He that loveth not knoweth not God; for God is love."* The Apostle admonishes the brethren to recognize that it is important to have

56

brotherly love amongst themselves, for this is the will of God. God had already instructed His people to love each other when he laid out His commandments. This is, therefore, His will: a beautiful gift of His grace and a way to enter His kingdom.

I am, therefore, not able to love someone without having the love of Christ within me. His love is more than a choice, for its richness and depth is beyond human comprehension. We will not be able to fully forgive someone and move on in love, unless God's love teaches us. In 1 Peter 1:22b, we are encouraged to: *"...love one another with a pure heart fervently."* Only Christ can purify our hearts and help us to rise above the normal, natural tendencies of being unforgiving.

"I've forgiven you, but I won't forget" is popularly used by people who have been hurt and want to demonstrate that they are attempting to forgive. But are we really exercising forgiveness, when we continue to revisit the past? It is very important that we learn from our experiences and use them as a tool for uplifting ourselves. On the contrary, if you find that you are still crying, still locking yourself away, still feeling bitter and angry every time you recall the events, then you have not forgiven. On the other hand, if we can think positively about our offenders, if we find pleasure in helping that person, if we are not devising a scheme to hurt them and if we are comfortable existing in the same space with that individual, then we know we have forgiven them.

While we strive for holiness, we will realize that forgiving is one of the hardest things to do. Forgiving is a complicated task that has to be intentionally worked on. It is hard because the hurt we feel is warranted but we must stop our hearts from rising sinfully against others. Our responsibility in holiness is to also check ourselves to see if we are responding negatively to certain situations. Having deep contentment in Christ is essential to have the emotional resources to respond with a forgiving heart. To be able to react lovingly and positively to someone that hurt us is a true gift from God and should be worked on to live without bitterness.

My experiences have taught me that:

- Love is pouring blessings on others, even when it is not warranted.
- Love is placing others above my hurt.
- Love is a smile that holds no grudges or lies.
- Love is peace that is poured from heaven's door.
- Love is sacrifice, despite your own emptiness.
- Love is fearless, when it seems like there is no hope.
- Love is wealth, when our finances are dry.
- Love is medicine that soothes various diseases.

For these reasons I hone love because it has the power to solve every problem that you can imagine. In my daily talk with God, I make an earnest effort to ask Him to teach me how to love, because I recognize that the way we demonstrate love is not in its truest form. Humans love
58

with expectations and conditions and, unfortunately, when people disappoint us and are not able to live up to those assumptions, then our "love" naturally diminishes. Sometimes it quickly turns into hate and discontent.

When we acquire spiritual love, we will learn to love unconditionally as God had intended. It is divine and can, therefore, only come from God. This spiritual love does not change as a person's situation changes; it satisfies others rather than ourselves.

MAKE LOVE YOUR PRIORITY

God's intention from the beginning is to lead a people who would mirror His character, which is love. This means while we continue to live busy lives and schedule our days, sharing love should also be our daily goal. Jesus emphasized the significance of giving love. He said in Matthew 22:37–39: *"Thou shalt love the Lord thy God with all thy heart, and with all thy soul, and with all thy mind. This is the first and great commandment. And the second is like unto it, Thou shalt love thy neighbour as thyself."* If we master these two commandments, all the other commandments would be easier for us to practice. Love fulfills the law and has the power to correct all the wrongs in the world today.

God must undoubtedly be the centre of starting your process of honing love. He alone can teach us how to love as we should. When we ask God to renew our minds, we should request that He gives us His thoughts. Thoughts left on their own are never pure, for bad thoughts are created by our fleshy nature. Sometimes we are victims of our thoughts, therefore, we need Jesus to renew our minds. If we always think that people set out to hurt us; if we always watch movies that portray bitterness; if we always have negative people around us who just gossip and if we always tell ourselves that no one likes us, then we are constantly feeding our minds with negative thoughts. If the thoughts are not pure, do not dwell on them. Thoughts will always come but we need to reject those that are not of God. When people think evil, they talk evil: *"...for out of the abundance of the heart the mouth speaketh."* (Matthew 12:34b). When we think bitter, then we act bitter.

Bitterness is an issue of the heart. It begins when someone does something to hurt us and when we perceive that someone has done us wrong. It is often concealed with pleasantries and smiles but is a deeply rooted emotion that is possibly devastating. Just as the roots of plants are widely spread and are hidden in the ground, so is bitterness when it finds footing in our hearts. Psychologist Dr. C. Wrosch explained in his research that: "Persistent bitterness may result in feelings of anger and hostility and if it is strong enough can affect a person's physical health." Wrosch highlighted that in an effort to deal with bitter emotions, individuals need to exercise the art of forgiveness.

Through God's grace we can replace bitterness with love. It is with the same heart that one believes on the Lord Jesus Christ, therefore, as one makes a conscious decision to allow God to rule over his/her life, then His grace will help that individual heal. *"For with the heart man believeth unto righteousness; and with the mouth confession is made unto salvation."* (Romans 10:10).

As we make a conscious decision to not only choose love and hone it, we must also give over our hearts to God.

NOTES

_____

_____

_____

_____

_____

_____

_____

_____

_____

_____

_____

_____

_____

_____

_____

_____

_____

_____

_____

_____

> **THE WORD OF GOD IS ALIVE AND POWERFUL! IT WILL SET YOU FREE, COMFORT YOU, HEAL YOU AND FEED YOUR SOUL.**
>
> ~ PASTOR MATTHEW HAGEE

chapter 6

Write Them Upon the Table of Thine Heart

od wants us to understand that He has given us the most powerful tool that can be used to rectify any situation in our lives. Men were always being inspired by God to keep records of life's changing experiences of many of our forefathers, specific words spoken by God and a tremendous number of prophecies to guide us into eternal life. The Bible has been given to us, not only as a book filled with laws or entertaining stories, but one that has been anointed by the Spirit of God. It changes lives one verse at a time. This book is a spiritual tool that has supernatural powers that can turn any darkness into blessed light.

In Luke 17:12-19, while Jesus was passing through Galilee, ten lepers saw Him and called out to Him for help. They were rejected and isolated, standing on the outskirts of the city and not able to have a normally functioning life. Their situation had brought them together, since they had nowhere else to go. They were scorned because of their disease and appearance.

The Bible states that they not only cried out to Jesus, but they also called Him "Master," which implies that they understood who He is and the power of His existence. Sometimes we see Jesus as our Lord, our Comforter in times of trouble, our Way Maker, and our Provider. Yet we refuse to see Jesus as our "Master," the One to whom we should surrender our all. We should give Him charge over our entire lives and make Him direct our paths and lead us into His glory. The lepers, in that desperate moment, gave Jesus complete charge over their affairs and, through faith, allowed Jesus to fix their problem. To be completely restored by God will be difficult, if we don't allow Him to take the role as our Master. What is that small thing that you have been holding on to? What secret hobbies do you have that are hard to step away from? Who is that person you are still upset with? What is that situation that is making you walk contrary to the will of God? What is that "thing" that is preventing you from calling out to Jesus, your Master?

It doesn't matter how low you fall or how hopeless the situation is, He will see you. He is a God who will see you in your despondent, miserable and unforgiving state. The lepers were hopeless before they cried out to Jesus and surrendered to His will. He became their master and because of this, they did not hesitate when Jesus instructed them to go to the priest. Though they were not immediately healed, Jesus knew that if they obeyed, their conditions would change by the time they approached the priest, who would give them clearance to re-enter into society. If we call out to Jesus, make Him our Master, and follow His Words, we will overcome our challenges. Once we follow God's directions, healing will take place. Seek after God through His Word.

As we aim to pursue God, it is never enough to only read or recite His Word, but we should inscribe the words of wisdom on our hearts and imprint them on our consciousness. Making His Word a part of our everyday lives and decision-making, will help us to fight the battles that we face. We must live, speak, and act the Word of God. Jesus reminds us that God wants us to be free from sin: *"The Spirit of the Lord is upon me, because he hath anointed me to preach the gospel to the poor; he hath sent me to heal the brokenhearted, to preach deliverance to the captives, and recovering of sight to the blind, to set at liberty them that are bruised."* (Luke 4:18).

God has been demonstrating to us that His Word is the key to unlocking His kingdom and to become beneficiaries of His sovereignty. We are often mesmerized by the thought of experiencing life in heaven. While this is where our minds should always be, God wants us to learn how to reach our ultimate home and have an enriched life here on earth. It is quite cliché to hear: "We all have a purpose here on earth," but how many of us seek God to unearth our unique God-given talent?

66

Our minds are usually busy thinking about the next big opportunity to seize, and we work towards self-actualization. As we grow and are promoted at different levels, we realize that the excitement is not lasting, so we move on to discovering the next venture to pursue and conquer. What if we could find our purpose, our calling: the single or many things that we were born to accomplish? I believe our lives would have superlative meaning. We would experience implacable joy and motivation; we would hunger after Christ and our souls consistently feed on Him.

This revelation comes from God's Word. When we seek Him and use what He gives to us, then our purpose(s) will become clear. *"Now the God of peace, that brought again from the dead our Lord Jesus, that great shepherd of the sheep, through the blood of the everlasting covenant, Make you perfect in every good work to do his will, working in you that which is wellpleasing in his sight, through Jesus Christ; to whom be glory for ever and ever. Amen."* (Hebrews 13:20 -21).

As we meditate on the Word, we must exercise faith for it to be hidden in our hearts. *"For unto us was the gospel preached, as well as unto them: but the word preached did not profit them, not being mixed with faith in them that heard it."* (Hebrews 4:2). God does not want us to hear the Word and believe they were only to illustrate Biblical characters. He has provided these examples and Scriptural references to help us as we navigate this life daily.

67

Believing that God will help others but not us is a big sign of lacking faith in Him. Our Father also wants us to accept the Word with humility, for in this state He will be able to transform our minds as the Word takes root in our hearts. *"Wherefore lay apart all filthiness and superfluity of naughtiness, and receive with meekness the engrafted word, which is able to save your souls."* (James 1:21).

Whenever we find ourselves feeling discouraged or lacking the strength to get over a disappointing situation, prayer will give us the boldness to persevere. Once the Word of God is hidden in our hearts, prayer will be our first impulse to overcome our situation. We will naturally want to cry out to God as our souls yearn for His grace. Ephesians 6:17-18 states: *"And take the helmet of salvation, and the sword of the Spirit, which is the word of God: Praying always with all prayer and supplication in the Spirit, and watching thereunto with all perseverance and supplication for all saints."* If we overlook the importance of making the Word a part of our existence, then confusion, doubt and stress will lead us to make foolish decisions that can intensify our problems. Prayer, coupled with the Word of God, is a robust strategy applicable in all circumstances of our lives, and our most downcast moments. He has encouraged us in His teachings to: *"Bind them continually upon thine heart, and tie them about thy neck. When thou goest, it shall lead thee; when thou sleepest, it shall keep thee; and when thou awakest, it shall talk with thee."* (Proverbs 6:21-22).

As effective as the "sandy loam" is to grow plants, so should our hearts grow with the Word of God. With this in mind, we want God to help us to prepare our hearts with all the right elements that will make it ready to receive the Word, nourish it, germinate it, grow it and then bear fruits from it. As we pray today, may we ask God, with sincerity, to prepare our hearts to obtain the Word and to help us use it for His splendour. We should not just study the Word for our personal gain or for vain repetition, but like David in Psalm 119:11, let us say: *"Thy word have I hid in mine heart, that I might not sin against thee."*

NOTES

GOD'S FORGIVENESS EXTENDS TO THE WORST OFFENDERS AND TO ANYONE WHO WISHES TO RECEIVE IT – NOT BECAUSE OF WHO WE ARE, BUT BECAUSE OF WHO HE IS.

~ CHARLES SWINDOLL

chapter 7

F.O.R.G.I.V.E: Father's Ointment Richly Given to Invalidate Vicious Emotions

urt, anger, strife, bitterness, contempt, animosity, maliciousness, wrath, rage, vindictiveness, spite, and hostility are just a few words that express our undesirable emotions toward an individual who has offended us in any way. Even the most trivial argument or disagreement can result in ill-feelings toward another person. These negative emotions are like quicksand that are known to trap and hold its victims with little room for escape.

As we continue to nurture the hurt that we experience, adverse feelings start to multiply and, before long, we are taken over by invasive thoughts that are hard to separate from. These feelings grow like wild venomous weeds that feed on and choke the life out of us. While we languish in our distresses, we continue to lose ourselves and often forget to show gratitude for the blessings we receive. We place ourselves in a position of barrenness, where our abilities to blossom and bear fruit are stifled.

Perhaps we foster these thoughts because we underestimate how vicious these emotions are and how necessary it is to guard ourselves against such unfortunate situations. God did not leave us alone to question the importance and necessity of forgiveness. He inspired the Psalmist to help us understand the need for us to forgive: *"If thou, Lord, shouldest mark iniquities, O Lord, who shall stand? But there is forgiveness with thee, that thou mayest be feared."* (Psalm 130:3-4). God reminds us that we are only living by His grace through forgiveness, as all would have been destroyed, if He did not grant pardon. Jesus re-enforced this when he was asked by Peter in Matthew 18:21-22 if he should forgive someone seven times, but Jesus' reply was that we must forgive *"seventy times seven."* Jesus was not concentrating on the mathematical calculation of these figures; He was simply imploring us to forgive as many times as it is required of us. In other words, we are admonished to keep shaking off the burden of un-forgiveness, in order to live a more fulfilling life.

"Come now, and let us reason together, saith the Lord: though your sins be as scarlet, they shall be as white as snow; though they be red like crimson, they shall be as wool." (Isaiah 1:18). God, through His love for each individual, has shown us that it doesn't matter how much we sin, He is willing to forgive us once we acknowledge our wrongdoing

and make a conscious decision to depart from our destructive ways. Just as the Samaritan woman that Jesus met at the well, who He forgave and set free, so is He calling and knocking on our hearts' doors waiting and willing to converse with us and set us free by the power of His forgiveness.

The cyclical nature of forgiveness is often misunderstood, but for us to understand its power, we should practise to forgive unconditionally. Forgiveness should not be bounded by the extent of one's infraction. Therefore, we are encouraged to forgive in every situation. Jesus taught us that while we forgive, God's hand of mercy will be extended to us. Let us remind ourselves of some of these New Testament Scriptures:

- ❧ "And forgive us our debts, as we forgive our debtors." (*Matthew 6:12*).

- ❧ "For if ye forgive men their trespasses, your heavenly Father will also forgive you: But if ye forgive not men their trespasses, neither will your Father forgive your trespasses." (*Matthew 6:14-15*).

- ❧ "And when ye stand praying, forgive, if ye have ought against any: that your Father also which is in heaven may forgive you your trespasses." (*Mark 11:25*).

- "And be ye kind one to another, tenderhearted, forgiving one another, even as God for Christ's sake hath forgiven you." (***Ephesians 4 :32).***

- "Forbearing one another, and forgiving one another, if any man have a quarrel against any: even as Christ forgave you, so also do ye." (***Colossians 3:13).***

God has told us that while it is important to worship Him, a believer must forgive before an attempt is made to do so. God also makes it clear that even if we know someone's heart towards us holds enmity, we should make all the effort to correct this situation before showing reverence to Him. Matthew 5:23-24 expresses this very well as Jesus explained to His disciples that: "*...if thou bring thy gift to the altar, and there rememberest that thy brother hath ought against thee; Leave there thy gift before the altar, and go thy way; first be reconciled to thy brother, and then come and offer thy gift.*"

We are not only unpleasant and choked up when we do not forgive but we undermine the task God wants to accomplish through us and we miss out on moments for God's glory to shine for others to come to Christ. Our Father knows just what we need, and forgiveness is His prescribed medicine to cure us spiritually, mentally and physically.

The remaining portion of this book will explore some benefits of our *"****F****ather's* ***O****intment* ***R****ichly* ***G****iven* ***to***

Invalidate Vicious Emotions." It is amazing what we can accomplish through Christ when we F.O.R.G.I.V.E.

NOTES

" " FOR BEAUTIFUL EYES, LOOK FOR THE GOOD IN OTHERS;
FOR BEAUTIFUL LIPS, SPEAK ONLY WORDS OF KINDNESS;
AND FOR POISE, WALK WITH THE KNOWLEDGE THAT YOU
ARE NEVER ALONE.

~ AUDREY HEPBURN

chapter 8

See the Good in Others

he kindness of a friend, spouse, colleague or loved one always seems forgotten when they have offended us. Sometimes all we process in that period is how we were mistreated. The act of betrayal that was carried out is now the pivotal retake of the movie that our minds display. Eventually all we can see is that individual in a negative light.

When we decide to forgive through Christ, we start to remember the good in the individuals who were mostly close to us. The more our focus is hinged on the good times that we had with the person, or some kind gestures that were extended to us, the more we will appreciate forgiveness. This is one way that will help us to heal.

The most vindictive person you know has a "soft spot," and has done some good deeds throughout his/her life, no matter how cold or cruel that individual may otherwise seem. Applying the Lord's antidote can help us to see the good in others, as we would have gained clarity of mind. It takes the grace of God to give us the courage to reopen our hearts to someone who has wronged us.

We are drawn closer to the heart of God when we can identify the good in others. Jesus displayed an astonishing level of compassion for those who society wrote off and treated less than human beings. Jesus, in Luke 7:50b, says: *"Thy faith hath saved thee; go in peace"* in reference to the woman who went to the Pharisee's house to see Jesus. The Bible explains that as she washed His feet with her tears and kissed His feet, the Pharisee questioned Jesus' authority in his heart as this woman was labelled a sinner. Jesus used her as a perfect example of how her faith made her more grateful than even His host, as she washed his feet and greeted Him with kisses, unlike the Pharisee. Here Jesus highlighted the good in her and how appreciative she was of His forgiveness.

At times we encounter situations where we treat people with disdain because they fail to live up to our expectations and have done things that do not represent God, themselves or their families. Usually those persons were once close to us and so the disappointment is felt greatly, but if we are able to look beyond those faults and recognize the beauty in them, it will fill our hearts and minds with the goodness of God. We can also learn more about ourselves from our positive outlook of others.

Some people are quick to repeatedly exclaim another's fault, ringing it through their ears and not recognizing that the individual can become confined to their past reality, and are unable to seek current opportunities to advance. As a child we use to say "sticks and stones will break my bones but words will never hurt me." However, as an adult I became more aware of the impact of people's negativity and, when the situation allows, I add a more positive perspective. It became more evident that "sticks and stones can break my bones and words can surely hurt." Words can be extremely damaging to people and we have to recognize that sometimes an individual needs a word of encouragement to strengthen them. I am not saying that you should ignore the error of their ways or not confront them. However, you should not use their offence as a prison, constantly reminding them of what they have done. Instead, you should provide emotional support by highlighting the good in them. Let them know how much you appreciate their effort as they seek to do something positive. Highlight some of their strengths and make them more aware of it. Perhaps they might not have noticed that they have such positive traits and will be encouraged to act differently and become better people. Remind them of who they are and what God has placed inside of them. Words of affirmation are simply emphasizing traits in the individual that already exist. Sometimes they need to hear it to display it.

Always looking at the positive in others will also reduce animosity, hurt, anger and resentment. Sometimes this mechanism does not only help the individual to feel forgiven and accepted but it acts as a testimony of the beauty that God has placed inside all of us. We are already winners when we look to see the good in others, as:

- Finding the good in others drives away the hurt we face.
- Finding the good in others defines the beauty of God.
- Finding the good in others preserves quality time spent together.
- Finding the good in others demonstrates love.
- Finding the good in others is synonymous with drawing closer to God.

NOTES

" BY HAVING A FORGIVING ATTITUDE, YOU CAN CHANGE
YOUR LIFE AND THE LIVES OF THE PEOPLE YOU CARE
ABOUT MOST.

~ KATHIE M. THOMPSON

chapter 9

Motivate Others to Love

hen we F.O.R.G.I.V.E, we demonstrate love to our offenders and ultimately heal our spirits. We essentially help to build our transgressor's character, while giving them a sense of peace. Although this might not be true in many cases, you will find that some people display love because of how it was extended to them. Love ignites love, which will continue to reciprocate and expand, even when we are not aware of it. We generally expect forgiveness to benefit the parties involved and help them move forward with gratitude and love.

It also helps those who are privy to the situation to be motivated to show love. The example you set will create a basis for them to feel free to forgive and love again. We might not consider the impact that forgiveness has on onlookers, but we must consider those individuals when we are faced with the choice to forgive.

Forgiveness was extended to Jacob by his twin brother, Esau, after Jacob deceived him and stole his birthright (See Genesis 25:27-34). This story related remarkable forgiveness that was witnessed by family members and servants. In Genesis 33, Jacob was afraid to see Esau after twenty years of hiding. He knew he had betrayed Esau and wondered if his brother would kill him. To Jacob's surprise Esau ran to him, kissed him on the neck and they wept (See Genesis 33:4).

Esau's journey through his recovery and growing intimacy with God was not recorded in the Bible. However, this phenomenal display of forgiveness is one that gives hope that our minds can be renewed, even in the worse circumstances. We can assume that Esau kept his faith in God and overcame unforgiveness when it mattered the most.

The opposite reaction is also a reality for many individuals who unintentionally cause others to stumble because of their lack of forgiveness. The Scripture reminds us in 1 Corinthians 8:9 that we should, *"...take heed lest by any means this liberty of yours become a stumblingblock to them that are weak."* When we display unforgiveness, we become hindrances in the spiritual development of those to whom we encounter. Our negative attitude is easily passed from one generation to the next, poisoning our children as they emulate this behavior. It also causes those who observe our unforgiveness to disrepute our Christian conviction and testimony. They may have been questioning their existence and have been seeking for refuge and change in Jesus but become discouraged because of your negative action being one who professes Christ.

*"**For God so loved the world, that He gave His only begotten son...**"* (John 3:16a), For God so "agape love" the world that He gave His only begotten Son, in my translation, is the love that God wants all of us to have. *Agape* (Pure/Selfless love) transcends *Philia* (Affectionate love), *Eros* (Romantic love) and *Philautia* (Self-Love). *Agape* is unconditional love that must be demonstrated, which God does every day. The Scripture says: *"while we were yet sinners, Christ died for us."* (See Romans 5:8). While we were in our sinful state, He showed us His love and, by extension, He forgave us.

As we look to God to help us experience His agape love, we must learn the art of forgiveness and demonstrate that one can progress beyond the hurt. When we truly give ourselves to people, we do not look for something in return and it is usually done when people are not deserving of it. Extending forgiveness to others who deserve otherwise is true agape love. God has given us unmerited love and forgiveness. His supernatural provision in our lives is greater than what we deserve, but He does it anyway and He does it with great joy and satisfaction. What a holy God we serve?

If we can get to that point where we sincerely forgive each other, then others will know Christ by our living. They too will have positive role models to follow. They too will live and learn how to forgive.

NOTES

"MAY GOD GIVE YOU...FOR EVERY STORM A RAINBOW, FOR EVERY TEAR A SMILE, FOR EVERY CARE A PROMISE AND A BLESSING IN EACH TRIAL. FOR EVERY PROBLEM LIFE SENDS, A FAITHFUL FRIEND TO SHARE, FOR EVERY SIGH A SWEET SONG AND AN ANSWER FOR EACH PRAYER.

~ IRISH BLESSING

chapter 10

We are Open to Newness in God

W hen we put our faith in God, we have peace in God. This newness in Him is undeniably the best place to dwell with God. The world's prosperity does not last, and it comes with sorrow and pain. The prosperity in God comes with no sorrow. God's newness will help you do the right things, even when the situation calls for something worse.

When David, and those who were loyal to him, fled from Absalom fearing for his life, he spent some time in the wilderness of Judah and, thereafter, crossed over the Jordon River as he returned to Jerusalem (See 2 Samuel 15:18). While in the wilderness, David had an encounter with God and it is theorized that it was in those moments that David penned Psalm 63, which still serves as peace and comfort to the souls of God's people.

David was brought to a very low place, having to face the betrayal of his son, who made it his duty to not only bring shame to his father but to kill him. In all the ordeal with Absalom and Ahithophel's struggles for power and revenge, and their intense efforts to destroy David, we witnessed how David's love for Absalom drew him closer to God. David instructed his men that Absalom should not be killed (See 2 Samuel 18:12) and the moment he found out that Absalom died, David wept for his son (See 2 Samuel 18: 33).

The fearless young lad, David, who slew Goliath, had soul-searching moments away from everyone, while he attended to his sheep. In those moments God was preparing him for seasons when he would be called a great King, a flawed fugitive, a warrior, a Psalmist and, most of all, **"a man after God's own heart."** Today, David remains one of my greatest heroes from the Old Testament Patriarchs, simply because he learnt the art of unlocking the true nature of God and opening himself to newness in our Heavenly Father.

David has taught me, through Psalm 63, that:

> ﹒ I must seek intimacy with God. My love for God must have depth and a persistent desire to be in His presence daily, not just on a coordinated worship day. *"O God, thou art my God; early will I seek thee: my soul thirsteth for thee, my flesh longeth for thee in a dry and thirsty land, where no water is; To see thy*

power and thy glory, so as I have seen thee in the sanctuary." (Psalm 63:1-2).

∾ I must worship Him just because He is God. Even if the walls around me are removed and it seems like all is lost, I must praise God because His awesomeness never changes, even when my circumstances change. *"Because thy lovingkindness is better than life, my lips shall praise thee. Thus will I bless thee while I live: I will lift up my hands in thy name."* (Psalm 63:3-4).

∾ I am conscious of the fact that my joy does not come from what the world has to offer and, even when I have no control over my problems, the joy of the Lord will remain within me. That is a gift from God. *"My soul shall be satisfied as with marrow and fatness; and my mouth shall praise thee with joyful lips: When I remember thee upon my bed, and meditate on thee in the night watches."* (Psalm 63:5-6).

∾ I must hide under the arms of God and know that He is my refuge and my everlasting strength. God's hands are enough to hold and shelter me from harm. In His hands is where I prefer to be than anywhere else. I am secured with Him. *"Because thou hast been my help, therefore in the shadow of thy wings will I rejoice. My soul followeth hard after thee: thy right hand upholdeth me."* (Psalm 63:7-8).

As I continue my journey with God, I thank Him for the many experiences, even those that were heart-rending that I endured over the years. My struggles in my early years allowed me to appreciate my many blessings today. I have had seasons where I withstood "Ahithophel Syndrome," while searching for my solutions to remedy my problems and simply ignoring the fact that I should take them immediately to God.

My problems seemed never-ending. As soon as I was able to breathe after an incident, another one arose, each with a fresh dose of hurt, frustration and annoying embarrassment. In my recollection of the past, I perceive that some of those situations were not directly my fights, but they affected my family/friends so, by extension, me.

Having become more mature in Christ, I have realized that God is my only true haven. It is more forceful now that I must decide to always choose love and make it a perfect gesture through Christ. As a steward of the Most High, I am encouraged by Him to F.O.R.G.I.V.E.

I challenge you to identify someone who has hurt you and make that decision, at this moment, to apply our **F**ather's **O**intment **R**ichly **G**iven to **I**nvalidate **V**icious **E**motions. I assure you that you will receive tremendous joy and grow spiritually. Where better can we find ourselves but to live in God's peace, reaping from the fullness of His joy, while preparing ourselves for better glory, in Jesus Christ our Saviour and King.

NOTES

" TO FORGIVE IS TO SET A PRISONER FREE AND DISCOVER THAT THE PRISONER WAS YOU.

~ LEWIS B. SMEDES

Conclusion

The compelling events of the life of King David have exposed us to the accounts of Ahithophel, who met his demise through a revengeful act against his King. Ahithophel's mind brought him to a state of feeling betrayed and bitter to the point where his thoughts were centered on hurting the person who destroyed his beautiful family. The depth of his hurt was as equal to his love for his family, which was uncontrollable and reckless. He lost all rationality, clinging to self and the appetite to avenge, while forgetting God and His perfect counsel. This condition is what I describe as "Ahithophel Syndrome" or as one who suffers from "Ahithophelia."

Ahithophel Syndrome describes the state of being of individuals who might be coping overall but have feelings of resentment or those who might constantly display sadness, despair and irritability; all choosing to deal with their own hurt instead of turning to the Lord for direction. Unfortunately, this may lead to us having that deep desire to get even with the people who have done us wrong. Such a state of mind only promotes darkness, which spreads around our beings and causes us to walk out of God's will and grace, resulting in death, whether physically or spiritually.

Ahithophel's behaviour stemmed from his refusal to forgive David. Unforgiveness is simply a matter of the heart, that if left untreated can make us ill in many ways. We may think we are doing well because we do not have to interface with our offender. However, once you have not forgiven such a one, your spirituality is being compromised.

David's problem was also a matter of the heart, while he created most of his problems and, by extension, enemies; his beloved son was resolute to destroy him. He too could have chosen to avenge his enemies but instead David ran to God and went through all the process necessary to F.O.R.G.I.V.E. He asked God for forgiveness, forgave himself, chose love, saw the good in Absalom, motivated others around him to love and was open to newness in God.

Be encouraged that you might feel alone but Jesus is riding out your storm with you and He will speak peace in your life and calm your storms. Even when your feelings are too painful to express, you need to remember that He understands the language of teardrops. Cry out to God and run to Him for refuge and sustenance. Remind yourself that your life is in His hands, therefore, you are not able to fix your problems. God knows all the answers and He will guide you through your situation with His perfect peace.

This book has demonstrated that there is a better way to deal with your vicious emotions. God can teach you to forgive so you can reap the benefits of it. Remember, forgiveness is not only for the wronged, but it was designed with you in mind.

About the Author

Diana Spencer is a dynamic and humble woman with a passion for life and helping others. Diana grew up in Kingston, Jamaica, where she attended the St. Andrew High School for Girls. She holds a Bachelor of Business Administration and a Masters in Business Administration Degree.

She has considerable experience in the Financial Sector, having worked for the Bank of Nova Scotia Jamaica and RIAS Insurance in the United Kingdom. She has lectured at the tertiary level at the University of the West Indies Open Campus and is now a Lecturer at the Caribbean Maritime University.

Diana is an ardent Christian who believes that life is meaningless without God at the forefront of all she does. She has various hobbies and has recently added a new interest to her collection. Her first book was birthed from an inspiration she received from God. With this book: **"Overcoming Ahithophel Syndrome: A Guide to**

Forgiveness," Diana aims to bless at least one individual with the words that the Almighty has placed on her heart. Diana is married with two children.

Bibliography

1. The Holy Bible: King James Version. Iowa Falla, IA: World Bible Publishers, 2001.

2. Bitterness Can Make You Sick, Rick Nauert PhD. August 2018.

3. Four Steps to Forgiveness, A Powerful Way to Freedom, Happiness and Success, William Fergus Martin, 2018. ISBN: 978-1-63443-344-0.

4. How to Actually Forgive Yourself, Caitlin Abber, 2019. https://www.oprahmag.com/life/a26028888/how-to-forgive-yourself/

5. The Cure for the Bitter Heart, Wayne Harrell, 2018 https://sermons.faithlife.com/sermons/212330-the-cure-for-the-bitter-heart

6. Eternal Life Ministries. "God's Word in Our Hearts," Thomas Manton. http://www.eternallifeministries.org/

7. Crosswalk.com. "The Power of Forgiveness," Cortni Marrazzo,2013. https://www.crosswalk.com/faith/women/the-power-forgiveness.html

8. Enduring Word. "Nathan Confronts David," David Guzik, 2018 . https://enduringword.com/bible-commentary/2-samuel-12/

9. The Man After God's Heart 1: A Heart of Hope, Melanie Newton, 2012. https://bible.org/seriespage/4-david-man-after-gods-heart-1-heart-hope

10. David the King, Bishop Barron, 2017 https://www.wordonfire.org/resources/blog/david-the-king-a-different-kind-of-bible-study/18354/

   IdleHearts (2020). Retrieved April 24, 2020 from https://www.idlehearts.com/

11. Paulo Coelh (2020). Retrieved April 24, 2020 from https://paulocoelhoblog.com/2011/04/07/old-hungarian-blessing/

12. BainyQuote (2001). Retrieved April 26, 2020 from https://www.brainyquote.com/quotes/thomas_carlyle_120684

13. PassItOn (2020). Retrieved April 26, 2020 from

https://www.passiton.com/inspirational-quotes/4126-its-not-about-how-much-you-do-but-how-much

14. Hagee Ministries (2020). Retrieved April 26, 2020 from https://www.jhm.org/DailyDevotional

15. John Hagee Quotes (2018). Retrieved April 26, 2020 from https://www.quoteswave.com/picture-quotes/321677

NOTES

NOTES

NOTES

www.ingramcontent.com/pod-product-compliance
Lightning Source LLC
Chambersburg PA
CBHW071454070426

42452CB00039B/1350